ON THE

Wings

OF

LOVE

Carol-Ann Moffitt-Neich

Paperback: 978-1-966652-06-9
eBook: 978-1-966652-07-6
Library of Congress Control Number: 2024926992

Ordering Information:

Prime Seven Media
518 Landmann St.
Tomah City, WI 54660

Printed in the United States of America

One day you will find the one
The one who looks at you
Like you're the only one on earth
The one who looks at you
Like they have never seen someone so beautiful
The one who looks at you
Like the stars shine just for you
The one who looks at you like
They can't believe you are theirs
The one who looks at you
Like they thank God every day
That you have come into their life
The one that you know you are safe
The one that you know you are loved
The one that you know you'll never
Have to look again
The one that is your home

The love one wants
The love one craves
Is but two hearts
That beat as one
Two souls
That dance together
A love of two hearts and souls
That melt into one

I see your smile
I look into your eyes
For your eyes tell me
How you really feel
I see the turmoil within
I see the dark storm
Beneath the smile
I see the dimness
Of your soul
If only you'd let me in
I would hold your soul
Tight against my heart
And bring the smile
From your lips
To your eyes

Don't be the one
Who broke her heart
Be the one who
Comes along and mends it
And makes her forget
It was ever broken

My heart is on fire
When your
Lips touch mine
You set it alight
Just looking into your eyes
You ignite it
At the very thought of you
The burning need I have
To have you in my life
Is something I have never felt before
Is something I can not douse
You have set my heart on fire
It's a flame
I never want to control
A flame
I never want to extinguish

You have stolen my heart
I don't know when you did it
I didn't feel you taking it
I just know you have stolen it

I would reach for the stars
Just to see them shine in your eyes
I would take the moon from the sky
To light the halo atop of you
For everyone to see the beautiful
Angel you are
I would steal the rays from the sun
To make sure you always felt
My arms giving you warmth
Even when I wasn't there
I would write your name in the sky
For you and the world to see
My love for you

Take the chance
Lay your heart on the table
Just maybe your love will come alive
But you'll never know
If you don't take the chance
Then your life shall begin
With all your dreams coming true

In case you didn't know
You are where my heart belongs
It doesn't belong anywhere else
But with you
Whether you are here
Or whether you are far
You always have my heart with you
For every day you hold my heart
Is a day I thank God
That he blessed me with you
Just wanted to tell you
In case you didn't know
In case I haven't told you lately

You are holding my heart hostage
I can't seem to move on
I have tried to
But I can't
You have my heart tethered to you
I can't see it
But I can feel it
My heart knows what it wants
And it wants you

I can't get you out of my head
You are constantly on my mind
From the moment I wake
Throughout the day
You are still on my mind
When I try and sleep
I don't know how to turn
My mind off
I don't know how to turn
My feelings off
I don't know how to get you
Out of my head
I don't know what is to become
Of these feelings
I don't know if they will ever
Dissipate
All I know is
You are living in my mind
You are living in my heart
I can't get you out of my head

Only you know what you feel
Only you know what's in your heart
Don't let anyone try and tell you
What to feel
What to think
You already have the answers
You know what's inside your heart
Trust your feelings
Trust your heart

I look at you
You reach out and touch me
That one touch
Holds so much emotion
So much love
I feel more alive
From your touch
Then I have in years
That one touch
Has sparked my heart
Has ignited my soul
Has set my body on fire
All from
Your one touch

You came in like a wrecking ball
You broke through my walls
You broke through my fears
You broke through my facade
You broke through my inhibitions
You came in and landed on my broken heart
With your wrecking ball
Determined to get to my heart
And show me what real love is

You have left your love on me
No matter how hard I try
I can't get over you
Your love lives in my heart
Your love lives in my mind
Though the distance seperates us
Your love is just there
I feel I could just reach out
And touch it
If only I could reach out and touch you
But no matter how hard I try
To get over you
Your love has left its mark on me
There's just no getting over you

I hold you tight
I breathe you in
Then I exhale
This is where
I should be
This is where
I belong

The beating of my heart
Increases whenever I think of you
Beats louder
When I hear your voice
Beats stronger
When your name leaves my lips
Beats faster
When I look into your eyes
The beating of my heart
Tells me what you mean to me
Tells me how much I love you
Tells me I'm alive
Whenever your around
Tells me
You are mine

One more night is all I want
Give me one more night
That's all I'm asking for
One more night to love you
One more night to hold you
One more night to kiss your lips
One more night to engrave
Memories of you
In my heart

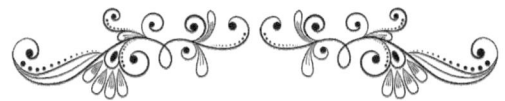

My heart has no space
For it is full
With my love for you
I feel it bursting
From my chest
Beating your name
With every breath I take
Reminds me
How blessed I am
To
Be walking this earth
With you by my side
Holding my hand
Along this journey
Through life

If I tell you
I love you
Know it's true
Know I mean it
Know it's from the heart
Just know
You are the only one for me
Just know
You are the only one I think about
Just know
I mean I love you
Forever

I am me
And you are you
We are but two
Who love
Two who become
Two souls entwined
Two hearts
That beat as one
But I am still me
Sometimes I am better
With you
Sometimes I am better
Just being me
Although we are perfect
Together
We are beautiful still apart
You are still you
And I am still me
And I will always be
Authenticly me
Never stop being you
Even when you are part of two

Age is but numbers put togehter
Some numbers mean more than others
The only number I care about
Are
1,4,3
I love you
The only numbers that matter
The only words that count

True intimacy
Is two minds
Two hearts
Two souls
That hear each other
That feel each other
That know each other
It's knowing each others
Goals
Dreams
Wishes
Thoughts
Fears
Insecurities
Love
It's our minds entwining
Before our bodies ever do

I look into your eyes
I feel like I'm drowning
I look at your lips
I just want them against mine
You hold my hand
I never want you to let it go
I step into your embrace
I want to stay there forever

I found a key
I'm now searching for the lock
I'm now searching for the heart
It unlocks
It's a very specific heart
It's a heart that beats in rythm
To mine
It's a heart that fits into my loving hands
Hands to hold it tight
Hands to protect it
Hands to unlock the love inside
So I'll keep searching
Until I find the right heart
The right lock
That my key unlocks
Forever open to me

In your eyes
I saw your past
I saw your pain
I saw your heart
I saw your beauty
I saw your soul
I saw your love
I saw my future
I saw my dreams
Coming true

You see faults
Faults in your ability
Faults in your intelligence
Faults in your looks
But to me, you are perfect
In my eyes, your mind enraptures me
In my eyes, you are so strong
In my eyes, your smile engulfs me
In my eyes, you are perfect
In my eyes, your imperfections
Are what make you even more beautiful
I wish you could see you
Through my eyes

Your whispered words
Are like brush strokes
On my heart
Every syllable
Adds to the piece of art
You are painting
On my heart
This is one art work
I hope
Never ends

Relationships aren't all love and roses
They are two people willing to put in effort
Effort everyday
To communicate, to compromise
To give and take
It's easy to just walk away
To blame the other person
It's hard to look in the mirror
And take responsibilities for your actions
For your words
And be willing to change, to
apologise, to make an effort
The right person makes you want
to do all this and more
The right person knows no ones perfect
The right person is wanting to make it work
The right person knows relationships
Take work and want to work together
Because that's what love looks like

I dream of you
In hopes that one day
That dream will come alive
No longer
Living inside
That you will see
My heart is open wide
For you are my dream
I hope one day
Will come alive

You are in my heart
You are the only one there
You have filled my heart
With your love
Don't ever think
I would ever have eyes
For anyone else
For my eyes only see you
Don't ever think there is room
For anyone else in my heart
My heart only beats for you
Don't think my soul speaks
To any other soul
For my soul sings
With every thought of you
There is no one but you
Never doubt my love for you
Never doubt
I love you

We don't get to choose
Who we fall in love with
Our heart chooses for us
But if I could choose
I would choose you
Over and over again

I chose you
You are my future
You are my best friend
You are my lover
You are the other half of my heart
You are the reason my soul sings
You are the reason I wake with a smile
You are the reason my days are filled with happiness
You are the reason my nights are filled with love
You are the reason I dream of a future
I choose you
Toady, tomorrow, and forever

You are the one for me
The one I dream about
The one that makes me smile
The one that makes my heart beat
The one my soul sings for
The one that makes my days brighter
The one that makes my nights sweeter
The one I want to wake up to
You are the one for me
The only one for me
Today, tomorrow, and always

Every time I think of you
I paint pictures in my mind
Pictures of happiness
Pictures of you
Pictures of a life of years to come
Pictures of a love so deep
That the canvas needs to be a wall
For I have so many memories and thoughts
Of our life and our love to come
That a canvas is just not big enough
To hold the love I have for you
So I shall paint my love for you
On a wall
For all to see
How beautiful you are
And how much love I have for you
Painted on my heart

I am me
You are you
Alone, we are unique
Together, we are
Unstoppable

I can't stop loving you
I know I should try
But my heart doesn't want to
My heart still beats for you
Though my soul misses you
My mind knows I'm just going to hurt
My heart by still loving you
But I just can't stop the love I feel for you
So if my heart doesn't want to
Then why should I
I'll just keep on loving you
Even if it's from afar

Our souls search for each other
They search this lifetime
Looking for their other half
For they know their soul
Is not complete with out their other half
So our souls search until they find it
So I will search until I find you
The other half of my soul
The other half of my heart
The other half of my life
One day I will find you

One day, you are going to be
Someone's dream come true
Someone who has been waiting
Their whole life
For you
For you have given
Your whole life to everyone else
It's now your turn
To receive the love
You have given everyone else
The love you thought
You would never find
Will find you
And be a love you have
Only dreamed about

I just know
Your heart
And
My heart
Are old friends
From long ago
That have found each other
Again

The warmth of you is what I want
The warmth of your smile
The warmth of your touch
The warmth of your hug
The warmth of your kiss
The warmth of your love
Can never be replaced
For you have warmed me
From my heart to deep into my soul
The warmth of you
Is all I need
Is all I want

When I say I love you
I love your mind
I love your laughter
I love looking into your soul
Through your eyes
I love the depth of your heart
Your kindness
Your empathy
Your loving heart
That's what I mean when I say
I love you

My heart is mine
Sometimes, I lose it
So if you find it
Cherish it
Don't throw it away
Because it won't be waiting
For you to find it again
You only have 1 chance
With my heart
For I know it's worth
I know when I love
It is with everything I have
So if you lose it
It will stay lost to you forever
You will never find a heart
Like mine again

If I give you my heart
Will you hold it
Will you love it
Will you treasure it forever
Will you never break it
Will you treat it like gold
Will you thank God we met
What will you do
If I give you my heart

You deserve someone who loves you
And means it
Who shows you how much they love you
You deserve to be the only choice
You deserve someone who will never leave
And know they never will
Because they show you everyday
You deserve a love
That makes you feel like a princess
Makes you feel you are the only one on earth
A love that you know that its not
always going to be easy
But a love that is easy to love
You deserve this
Don't settle for anything less

What we want
Is someone who simply says
How was your day
I'm here for you
We can work it out
We can do it together
It'll be alright
I love you

You could be the one sent from above
Just for this person
To show them what love is
To make them feel worthy
To make them feel loved
But just because you love them now
It just may not be the right time for them
You may be there before they have healed
Before their heart is ready to
recieve all you have to give
You may just have to take a step back
If you are willing to wait
If they are the right one for you
You will wait
Forever
If that is what it takes

You're my weakness
You're my kryptonite
You're my Superman
You're my happiness
You're my joy
You're my light
You're my love
You have my heart
You have my soul
You have my life
You have my everything
You are my everything

Love is supportive
Love is not controlling
Love is holding your hand
Love is going for a drive
Just to spend the time together
Love is there to congratulate you
on your acheivments
Love is there to hold you in time of trouble
Love is there to laugh at your silly jokes
Love is there to hold you when the sun goes down
Love is there to smile at you when you wake
Love is what you see when you look into their eyes
Love is what you feel when your
head is on their chest
Their heart beating your name
Love is not wanting to imagining a life without them

People strive for riches
They work hard
Day after day
I strive for the riches
In your heart
I'll strive day after day
Just to see you smile
Just to know you are happy
I'll work hard
Year after year
For the love
Between you and I

I know somewhere there is someone for me
I search this world looking for you
Wondering if our souls will call to each other
When we meet
Will you feel my heart beating for you
Will I feel the pull of you
Will I look into your eyes
And just know
You are the one
I have been searching for
Will this lifetime be the one
We are meant to reach out
And never let go
Will the calling of our souls
Call so loud that we can't help
But find each other
So this search will end
End with two hearts becoming one
Two souls finally at peace

I saw you
My soul felt you
My heart beat for you
My eyes cried for you
My smile brightened
My mind began to wonder
Though I had never met you
My soul knew you

I see you
I can't stop looking
I can't stop thinking about you
I think about you as the sun goes down
As I make my way to bed
I just know I will lie there for hours
As sleep eludes me
Just thinking of you
Wondering if you are thinking of me too
When finally sleep engulfs me
My dreams are filled with you
Filled with your smile, filled with your eyes
Filled with a life only I imagine with you
I wake, my first thoughts are of you
My mind doesn't stop
It is always filled with thougths of you
I can't explain this addiction to you
Maybe one day
You can explain it to me

My phone chimes
A smile automatically appears
Just with the excitement that maybe it is you
A message from you is enough to get me excited
Any message
Just says you are thinking of me
I love that chime
I wait for that chime
I can't get enough
Of that chime
I can't get enough
Of you

Every word counts
Every word I speak
Are words that come from deep within
So, know every word I whisper
To the stars
Every word I have dreamt
That I tell you in my dreams
Every word I have thought
Throughout the day
Every word I speak to you
Are words of love
That comes straight from
My heart
Every word that finds you
Are words I have prayed to God
That one day
I would be able to tell you
Of this love I feel for you
From deep with in my heart
From deep with in my soul
These words I whisper to you
These words of my love
I prayed for so long
One day
I would be able to give you
Are words that no longer will be
Just words
But a ribbon of love
To wrap around your heart

Every day is a new day
With you
Every day is the begining
Of the rest of our lives
Every day is the first day
On repeat
Every day love has blessed me again

You say you're not perfect
I say who is
I say there is not a person alive
Without faults
I say your imperfections
Make you who you are
In my eyes I think you are beautiful
I say your imperfections
Made you the person
Who always has a smile
Who laughs hard
Who gives without expectations
Who loves with all their heart
I say you imperfections
Are infectious
You say you are not perfect
But I say, you are perfect for me

If you are lucky
Someone will come into your life
Who will turn your life around
Show you what it's like to be truly loved
A love so deep and pure
A love you thought never really existed
Only in fairy tales
A love that you never want to live without
If you are lucky
I hope this kind of love
Finds you

In every whisper of the trees
I hear your name
Calling out to me
In every step I take
Takes me one step closer
To you
In every sunset I see
Is another day of beauty
I see reflected of you
In every star that shines
Shines for you
To illuminate my love
Every sunrise
Is another day
That warms my heart
I see beauty all around
I see you everywhere I look
I feel you in every breath I take

Your scars are not scars
They're tracks
Where my love can travel
So the more scars
The more my heart
Can follow
The more tracks
My love can travel

When I say I love you
I love all of you
I love you through the ups and down
I love you with all my heart
Like I've never loved anyone else
I can't imagine a life without you in it
I can't wait to spend the next 50 years
Waking up next to you
Sleeping in your arms
When I say I love you
I mean I love you
Unconditionally
I mean I love you forever

I see your lips
I want to kiss them
I look into your eyes
I see my furture
I hear your words
They melt my heart
I touch your hand
My body starts to tingle
From your touch
I step into your embrace
I am home

The right person
Will lift you up
Will inspire you
Will encourage you
Will hold your hand
Will be your biggest cheerleader
Will make you want to be the best version of you
Will bring a smile to your lips
Will have you thanking God every day
For bringing them into your life
The right person
Will love you
Will always make it known
Just how much you mean to them
You will just know
They are the
Right person for you

Love that's meant for you
Will find you
And bring so much with it
Bring a smile to your lips
Bring life into your eyes
Bring a glow to your heart
Bring arms to hold you tight
Bring words to engulf your soul
Bring life back into your world
Bring everything you thought
You lost

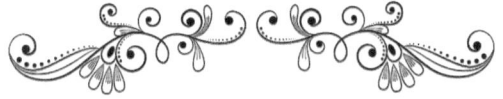

You gave me a reason to smile
A smile you had never taken away
You held my hand
A hand you never dropped
You gave my mind peace
A mind you never were at war with
You healed my heart
A heart you didn't break
You mended my soul
A soul you didn't destroy
You believed in my dreams
Dreams you never crushed
You brought me back to life
A life I now love again
You are the love
I will never stop loving

If I follow you into the sunset
Where will you lead
Will you look back for me
Will you hold your hand out
If I fall behind
Will you want this time to ever end
Tell me
If I follow you into the sunset
Will the sun go down on our love
Or will the moon take over
And show us the way

You've made my heart smile
Do you believe a heart can smile
I never did
Until you made it happen
Now I'm sitting here
A smile on my lips
And can feel my heart
Smiling
With the very thought of you
You can't see either
You may never know this
But that's ok
Because my heart smiling
Will last me a lifetime

Have you ever met a stranger
But feel you already know them
Your heart beats faster
Your soul starts to sing
You can't stop smiling
Your mind can't stop
You know
You just met
Your soul mate
I hope one day
This is your story

I want my words to touch your mouth
And bring a smile to your lips
I want my words to touch your mind
And bring you happiness
I want my words to wrap around your heart
And make you feel loved
I want my words to bury deep into your soul
And touch your soul with peace
I hope you feel my words
I hope they are bringing
A smile to your lips
Happiness to your thoughts
Love to your heart
Peace to your soul
I hope my words
Touch you
Whenever, wherever
You need them

You just need that one person
To hug you
Like no one ever has
That hug, that makes
All your broken pieces
Just meld back together
To make all the broken
Memories
Just fade away

Love is on it's own time
You can't schedule it
You can't spend your life
Waiting for it
You can't predict it
You can dream about it
You can wish for it
But you can never wait for it
For love
Is on it's own time
It will come to you
When it's ready
When you need it the most
When you least expect it

You can fall in love
Before you ever meet
Fall in love with their mind
Fall in love with their voice
Fall in love with their words
Fall in love with their kindness
Fall in love with their heart
Fall in love with their soul
That has touched yours
Without a single look

Don't waste your words
When you say
I love you
Mean it
Don't waste those words
For those words
Are not something to be thrown around
They my be tiny in letter count
But migthy in meaning
The mightiest of all words
That have ever been spoken
So when they leave your lips
Make sure they leave with meaning
Make sure they leave with truth
Don't waste them

My eyes saw you
Saw your beauty
Saw your smile
Saw your eyes shining
But most of all
My eyes saw your heart
That's when my heart
Fell in love with you

There's you
Then there's me
We can be
An us
If you let it be
For 1 plus two
Maybe makes three
But it only makes
A we
Regarding you and me
So we can
Be an us
Only if you let it be

My heart beats for you
My soul sings for you
My thoughts pray for you
My life is better with you
In it
Never forget
The love I have for you

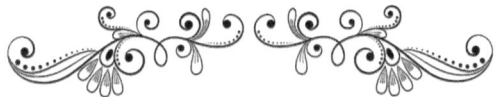

Then you were there
Standing in front of me
A stranger
Who was to become
Someone I can't go a day without
Someone I can't wait to hear from
Someone I can't wait to see
Someone I can't wait to have in my life
Each and every day
Each and every moment
One day a stranger
Then, the next, someone
I can't live without

When I see you looking at me
I feel like I'm melting
Like the sun has come out
And shone just for me
My heart beats faster
A smile crosses my lips
Happiness floods my soul
From just one look
That one look
Is magical

Walking along the waters edge
I look behind
To see the footprints left behind
The waves that awash by me
Wash away my prints
But unlike my footprints
The footprints you left
On my heart
Will never wash away
For although we walk
By different waves
We walk along the same ocean
An ocean full of memories
Of a love you left behind

As sure as the sun goes down
As sure as the moon disappears
You can be sure
My love will never go down
My love will never dissapear
My love will always shine
For you
Day and night
For that
You will always be sure of

I see you
I see the real you
Know if I fall for you
I fall for you
I fall for your heart
I fall your soul
I fall for your kindness
I fall for you with my heart
For my heart sees you
I don't fall for you with my eyes
My eyes can't see your heart
But my heart
Sees yours
My heart feels yours
So know
If I fall for you
I see you
I see the real you

The clouds are heavy
The sky is dark
Rain threatens
But not to me
For I look at you
And I see the sun
Shining down
My heart is smiling
Brighteneing my day
For you make everyday
Shine

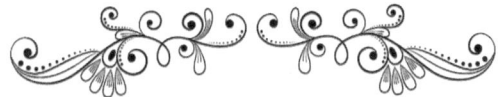

I hope one day you'll find the one
The one that only wants to see you smile
The one who makes you feel safe
The one you makes your heart beat louder
The one who texts you first
The one who wants a life together
The one who wants you to be just you
The one you know won't give up
The one who just makes everything right
The one who loves you
Just as much as you love them
One day
I hope you find
The one

I feel you pulling
Feel you pulling
On my heart
Even when I can't see you
Even when you
Are not near
With just the thought
Of you
I feel you
Pulling
On my heart

Loving you to the moon and back
Never waivers
Sometimes the moon is close
Sometimes the moon
Is nowhere to be seen
Sometimes it's a cresent moon
Sometimes it's a full moon
No matter what shape
No matter how far it is
My love for you never waivers
Though the moon is ever changing
My love does not
My love is ever present
Ever shining for you

I have fallen for you
I fell for your eyes
I fell for your smile
I fell for your mind
I fell for your heart
It's a fall
I'd gladly fall
Over and over again
Every day

My soul was hungry
Hungry with need
My heart was thirsty
Thirsty for love
My mind was full
Full with hope
My arms were empty
Empty of you
My eyes were looking
Looking everywhere
For what they needed
What they needed to see
Was you

In my eyes
You are amazing
In my eyes
You are incredible
In my eyes
You are beautiful
In my eyes
You are perfect
In my eyes
You are my forever

What love looks like
To me
A single rose
Says more than dozens
A night at home
Wrapped in your arms
By the fire
Listening to music
A drive
To sit by the water
And watch the moonlight
The headlights shining
With us dancing
In the light
A picnic
Under a tree
With a basket full
Of love
That's what love
Looks like to me

You hold your hand out
I place mine inside
I feel happy
I feel safe
I feel loved
I feel whole
I feel blessed
It fits perfectly
I am home

Your heart
Your beautiful heart
Is all I need
For your heart is priceless
No amount of money
No amount of beautiful faces
No amount of riches
Could ever come close
To your heart
For your one heart
Is worth more than money can buy
Is worth more than any fleeting moment
For your one heart
Is all I'll ever need

I feel you

I feel the pull you have on my soul

I am unable to resist

Though

That does not matter

For my soul

Has no power to run

Only a need

To be connected

To yours

You've turned a light on
In my heart
A light I thought
Would never burn again
The flame you have ingnited
Burns brighter
Everytime I think of you
Burns hotter
Everytime I see you
You have ignited
An ever burning flame
Of light
With your love
That has touched my heart
Touched my soul
Has turned my light on
Has rekindled the light
In my heart
Has rekindled the life
In my soul
I had thought
Had long burnt out

My heart weeps for you
But do not concern yourself
As it does not weep in sorrow
But in love
A love it never thought
It would ever find

My heart is my compass
Leading me to you
Leading me dircetly
To your heart
I will blindly follow
The direction it leads
For a compass
Never gets lost
For a compass
Never leads you
In the wrong direction
I will always follow
Where it leads
Because it led me
Directly to you

Your words sing ot me
Like a morning bird song
Your words gently whisper to me
Like a breeze whispers to the leaves
Your words wrap around my heart
Like arms that hold me tight
Your words penetrate my soul
Like rays of sun that warm my skin
Your words give me life
Every word you speak
Breathing life back into
My soul

I want to hold your heart
I want to be the one
That makes your heart
Beat a little faster
I want to be the one
Who makes your heart
Swell with love
I want to be the one
Your heart knows
Will love you forever
I want to be the one
Who mends all
The broken pieces
I want to be the one
You know is safe
I want to be the one
Who fills your heartache
With my love
I want to be the one
You give your heart to
I want to be the one
To hold your heart
And never let it go
I want to be your one

Every day I wake
I thank god
Not because I wake
But because
I wake next to you
Every day I get to see you
The first person I see
When I wake
I get to fall in love with you
Every morning
All over again

I feel you pulling

Pulling me to you

Pulling on the string of love

Though I may try to pull away

Stretching the string

But never letting go

Then at times you pull it

As you run

It never breaks

No matter how far away

No matter how tight we pull

No matter how fast we try and run

It never breaks

For our destinany is you and I

To be forever

Together

As one

I walk along the moonlit path
Looking above
Looking for a shooting star
To catch for you
So I'll take that star
And place it in your hands
For you to make all
Your dreams come true
For I do not need it
For I already have it all
With you

I'm jealous of the wind
That touches your lips
I'm jealous of the sun
That warms your heart
I'm jealous of the stars
That shine in your eyes
I'm jealous of the moon
That lights your soul
I'm jealous of the flowers
That you hold in your hands
I'm jealous of the dandelion
That you make a wish on
I'm jealous of the one
Who gets to hold you tonight

Laying here
In your arms
Is where I belong
As you are forever
In my heart
Where you will
Always belong

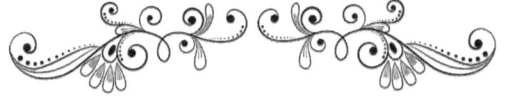

I look at you from afar
And see your smile
I look at you from afar
And see your eyes sparkle
I look at you from afar
And see your lips moisten
I look at you from afar
And see your heart beating
I look at you from afar
And love you close to my soul
I look at you from afar
Because loving you from afar
Is better than not loving you
At all

Someone who loves you
They wont even feel the rain
They only feel your soul
And what you need
So they won't even notice
The rain falling down on them
They will only want
To be your umbrella

And when my days
Come to an end
When my heart stops beating
My soul shall look for you
In the next life time
For this love
Had no begining
And knows no end
It was just always there
Where it belonged
Where it was always
Meant to be
Between
You and me

I was lost
Then you came along
Helped me find me
Find my smile
Find my laughter
Find hope
When you are lost
Find the one
Who helps you find
You agian

I want to listen
To your strories
I want to hear
All the stories your heart
Has to tell
I shall rest my head
Against your chest
And listen until your
Hearts content
For every story
Your heart wants to tell
Is a story
My heart just wants
To love a little bit more

Cheek to cheek

Lip to lip

Heart to heart

Soul to soul

Is the only way

I want to feel you

The only way I want to feel

Love

You were the one
The one I saw
Forever holding hands with
Forever laughing with
Forever laying with
Forever dreaming with
Forever dancing in the
Moonlight with
Forever talking into
The night with
Forever kissing
The one I saw myself
Growing old with
I thought I had found
The one

If my heart calls your name
Will you answer
If my soul sings to yours
Will you harmonise
If my hand reaches for you
Will you reach out
If my lips touch yours
Will you smile
If I wish for everlasting
Will you engulf us
Forever

Find the one
You want to put up christmas lights with
Year after year
The one you want to hold hands with
While drivng along
The one you want to kiss in the middle of the night
When you wake for no reason
The one you want to share your day with
Just to know they care
The one you can sit and just be you with
Just listening to music by the fire
The one you want to go on long drives with
To desintations unknown
The one you want to tell your dreams to
And have them tell you, you can do it
The one you want to still be
holding hands at 90 with
With love still in your eyes
You just need to find your one

Mountains have moved
The stars have aligned
The sun has shone brighter than ever
You are an answer to my prayers
I have prayed for a love so true
And God replied
With you

Your love takes me
All the way to the moon
I feel like I'm flying high
Through the stars
That I see reflected
In your eyes
Burning into my heart
Deeper than anyone
Has ever gone
Higher than
I have ever felt
A love that sings
To my soul

You are my bright light
You are my light to end my darkness
With you I see the light shinning through
With you I see darkness coming to its end
With you I see a future filled with
a forever shinning glow
I see days filled with happiness
Nights filled with love
A future filled with a life time
Of memories to hold

I hope you find someone
Who loves you just as you deserve
For you deserve a love
That treats you with respect
That treats you with honesty
That treats you like you are the most
Amazing person they have ever met
That makes you feel safe
That makes you feel love like
You've never felt
That makes you feel like you are
The only person they see
That makes you feel you have
Just stepped into a movie
I hope you find the love of a lifetime
Because you desereve that
And nothing less

You have
Marked my soul
A mark that is not erasable
A mark that will be there for
Life
A mark that must be tattooed
For I can not forget you
A mark I shall cherish
For a lifetime to come

You touched my soul
But if I let you touch my heart
Only touch it with love
Please don't leave anything behind
There is already too much
Weighing it down
Too much I'm slowly removing
Bit by bit, day by day
Memories of a past
I'd rather leave behind
So touch my heart
With hands of love
And a promise of tomorrow

Once upon a dream
I dreamt of a love so true
I dreamt of dancing under the moon
In the arms of a love so pure
I close my eyes as I feel demure
As we sway
I feel like we are in a land
Far, far away
Just you and I
Dancing like a dream
Come true

Love is worth waiting for
Love of a lifetime
Not a love just to fill in
A love that makes you feel safe
A love that consumes your heart
A love that makes you feel free
A love that although you are together
You also feel free
Free of worry
Free of control
Free of manipulation
Free just to love
To love each other
To love you
To love life

You just need that one person
To love you
The way you didn't know
How to love yourself
The way you didn't know
You deserved
The way you have never
Been loved before

When I think about the rainbow
I think about the pot of gold
What is in that pot
What is that pot of gold
Is it a thing
Or could it be a person
I wonder what is in my pot of gold
What will I find
Though I stop and think
I have already found my pot
The day you came into my life
I don't think I could find anything
More precious than you
So when I see the next rainbow
I'll pray that you find your pot of gold
That is waiting just for you
Just as I have found mine

You are my heartbeat
Without you
My heart has no reason
To beat
No reason to love
Without you
My heart would just stop
You are my forever
Heartbeat

I see you everywhere
I close my eyes
It's you, I see
Looking back at me
In my dreams
And in my thoughts
Your smiling face
Is all I can see
What does this mean
When you are not mine
But you are everywhere
It seems
Looking like a dream
Looking back at me

From the moment we met
I realised why my heart
Had a beat

The fire that burns
Deep within my soul
Is eternal
Looking not for the one
To extinguish it
But for a love
To keep the flame
Burning
Forever more
With a love
That flickers
Night and day
With just one touch
Deep within my soul

Do you know how you have change me
Changed the way I view love
Love now seems close
Close enough to touch
Touch it with my heart
Heart and soul
Soul deep love I can touch
Touch with every pore
Pour my heart and soul into loving
Loving you

Some people exist

Just

So they can breathe

Life back

Into the souls

Of the ones

They were created for

The ones

Where no matter where

No matter how long

They will always find their way

To them

For the connection

Was always meant to be

Never to be broken

But always to be found

My heart will be forever marked
With your name
Your smile
Your love
A mark that cannot be erased
Nor do I even want to try
For the memories of you
Are what hold my heart together

You don't just feel like home
You are my home
You are where I lay my head
You are where I feel safe
You are my warmth
You are my peace
You are where I feel loved
Wherever you are
That's where my home is
You are my home
You are the lock
My key fits

As I lay here wrapped in your arms
My head against your chest
I reach up and kiss your sweet lips
Before going to sleep with a smile on my face
I wake still wrapped in your arms
Our bodies entwined
Smiling as I'm not dreaming
I'm laying here in our love

When I see you
I see the real you
I see beneath the surface
I see into your heart
I see everything you don't see
I see everything you don't feel
I see the beautiful soul within
I see everything you think you're not
I see the hurt buried within
I see the heart just wanting to be loved
I see the one I just want to hold tight
And tell everything is going to be alright
Everything is going to work out
You are worth being loved
You are worth loving
You are loved

I love how you take me in your
arms and dance with me
Dance to the beautiful melodies
playing in the distance
Dancing under the stars
No one watching
Just the two of us
Swaying to and fro
Feeling your heart beat against mine
Kissing under the stars
Wishing the night will never end
Two souls dancing in the moonlight

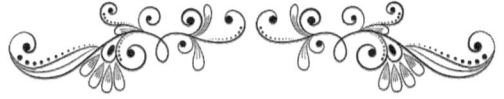

My heart sings with joy
My mind hesitates
My hands shake
My upper lip glistens
My mind cries out
My heart screams with need
Will my heart win
Or will my mind dominate
Will I cry tears of joy
Or tears of sorrow
My heart is fighting hard
To be victorious
For the love
It sees
For the love
It needs
The cost my mind pleads
Is worth everything
My heart has already
Planted the seeds

I dream when we will be together
Together to touch your face and kiss you
To sit together with your arms around me
With my head on your chest
Sitting in the bliss of our love
Talking about our day
Talking about the future
Talking about our dreams
Sitting with the love of my life

The book of life
Could not be written
Without you
My days are engulfed
With thoughts of you
As you immerse yourself
Into my slumber of dreams
Not a page could be written
Without words of love
Without thoughts of a time
Where pages have no meaning
Where life of long ago
Pages meant nothing
Without you

Love is something we search for
We search for our other half
We look for a soul to complete ours
In a planet with billions of souls can we
ever find the one who completes us
If you are one of the lucky ones your souls
will cross paths and find each other
That one soul
Who completes you forever

This feeling of love
Where does if come from
How can you truly explain this feeling
It just is
Love is not a feeling
Love is not an action
Love is not just a word
True love is all consuming
Consuming every thought
Consuming every dream
Consuming your days
Consuming your nights
Consuming your mind with the love of your life
That one person who completes you
That one person you want to spend
the rest of your life with

I walk the streets with a smile
People smile back
They smile but don't know why I'm smiling
They can't see into my heart and soul
They have no idea you are the reason
I walk this earth thanking God everyday for you

As I sit and ponder life's journeys
My mind wonders to you
To your eyes
To your lips
To your heart
To your soul
My lifes journeys has led me to you
How long will my journey with you be
Will it be a week
A month
A year
A life time
Only time will tell
Only time knows

My heart feels so full
Full from the love you send me
Full of the love I have for you
There's no better feeling in the world
Then walking around with a full heart
Filled with love

I think you have been sent from above
You are my shinning light
My light that has lightened my heart
A heart that was once shattered and closed
Which you have come and mended and
opened with your love and light
You are my angel
My angel of love
Come to love and cherrish me
What a blessing you are my love
Wrap your arms around me my angel
As I could never imagine being
anywhere else but in your arms
My love for you is never ending
I love you today, tomorrow and forever

I want to be that couple that
everyone is talking about
The couple that everyone sees the love between us
The couple who walks around holding hands
The couple who can't stop smiling
The couple who can't stop kissing each
other and doesn't care who sees
The couple who just knows how lucky
we are to have found each other
The couple they write about
The couple who truly loves forever

Though we are oceans apart
The miles seperate us
Our love is close to our hearts
Love makes the distance dissipate
My love comes from deep within
A line of pearls of love connecting my soul to yours
That pull
Pulling us together
Pulling through space and time
Pulling until our hearts become one
Where no one else compares to the man you are
You are the only man for me
My best friend, my confidant my everything
The love of my life
I'm blessed and thank God for you everyday
For a day without you is a day I don't want to live
You are my everything
I love you
Our love is forever

I hear your words though I don't hear you
I see your love though I don't see you
I feel your soul though I don't feel you
You have invaded my mind
Body and soul
With love

I love you so much
I just dream of the days and nights together
I want to lie in bed with you with my head
on your chest listening to your heartbeat
I want to lay together and talk about our day
I want to reach up and kiss your beautiful face
I want to tell you I love your beautiful face
I want to tell you I love you over and over again
I want to fall asleep in your arms
with a smile on my face
I want to wake up next to you and know
that the day ahead is going to be another
blessed day with you in my life

Only time will tell where the journey will lead us
For there is no time limit on love

Can you see how your words are touching my heart
Can you see how your love is touching my soul
Can you see how I'm falling for you
Can you see how you make me smile
Can you see how you make me laugh
Can you see how much I love you

I think I'm obsessed
Obsessed with your words
Obessed with your mind
Obsessed with your eyes
Obsessed with your smile
Obsessed with your talent
Obsessed with your love
Obsessed with you

How can you touch my soul when
we haven't touched hands
How can you make me see love when I look in
the mirror when we have never seen each other
How do I see love in my eyes when
I've never looked into your eyes
How does my heart beat fast when
I've never felt your heart beat
How do I long for your words when
I've never heard your voice
How do I dream of you when I have never seen you

I love the way you make me smile
I love the way you make me laugh
I love the way you are getting into my soul
I love the way you have invaded my heart
I love the way you make plans for us
I love the way you make me feel special
I love the way you make me feel
I'm the only one
The last one

I'm afraid to tell you how much I love you
I'm afraid to let you in
I'm afraid to tell you my secrets
I'm afraid to let you into my soul
I'm afraid to fall
I'm afraid to beleive this is real
I'm afraid to trust you
I'm afraid I'm not enough
I'm afraid not to love you
I'm afraid you won't love me
I'm afraid not to have you in my life
I'm afraid to let go of my inabitions
I'm afraid to trust the universe has got this
I'm afraid of losing you
I'm afraid but I love you so much
I'm taking a leap of faith

Love is patient
Love is forgiving
Love is accepting
Love is kind
Love is trusting
Love is honest
Love is soft
Love is holding a heart in your hand
Treating it like the most precious thing in the world

I wake up, I think of you
I wonder what you're doing
I wonder what you're thinking
I listen to our songs
I wonder what you're doing
I wonder what you're thinking
I look at my phone
I wonder what you're doing
I wonder what you're thinking
I go to bed I think of you
I wonder what you're doing
I wonder what you're thinking
I wonder if you're thinking of me as
much as I am thinking of you

How can I feel this so quickly
How have you touched my heart so fast
How have you invaded my every waking hour
How have you captured my dreams
How have you given me hope again
How can I live without you in my life now
I hope I never have to

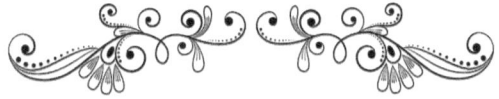

Can you feel my love
Can you feel my love across the ocean
Can you feel my love across the skies
Can you feel my love across space
Can you feel my love in the air
Can you feel my love in the whisper of the trees
Can you feel my love in the breeze across your face
Can you feel my love when the
sun beats on your skin
Can you feel my love when you look at the moon
Can you feel my love when the stars shine above
Can you feel my love all around you day and night

Can this be real
Can you really be the one
I never knew I needed
Can the distance be overcome
Can the love we feel be real
Can the bond we share never break
Can we be lost souls yearning for each other

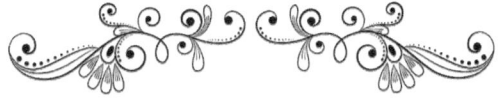

Love

My love

I love you

I love your heart

I will always love you

I will always love your essence

I will always love your eternal soul

I will always love the person I know

I will always love what you have shown me

I will always love what you have blessed me to see

I will always love you to the

moon and stars and back

You are thousands of miles away
Yet I feel you all around me
You are thousands of miles away
Yet I feel the connection attaching us
You are thousands of miles away
Yet I feel you thinking of me
You are thousands of miles away
Yet I feel you loving me

Love
What is love
Are we in love with the thought of love
Is it the feel of someones arms wrapped around you
The taste of someones lips pressed against yours
The feel of someones body entwined with yours
The feel of someones mind connected to yours
Is it all of these things
Or is it the thought of
Never seeing them again
Never hearing their voice again
Never feeling them again
The thought of not being able to breathe
Not being able to live without them
Or is it all of these things

My tears tell me how much you mean to me
How much I have missed you
But most of all how much I love you

What started as hello
Is finishing with I love you
I will always love you
You are my everything
I don't know how to breathe without you
I can't live without you
I don't want to live without you
I am in love with you

I hear the ding
I get excited
I see your name
My heart races
I read your message
My heart explodes

Love
You can't see it
You can't hear it
You can't taste it
You can't touch it
Or can you
You can see it in the eyes of your loved one
You can hear it from the lips of your loved one
You can taste it from the mouth of your loved one
You can touch it from the heart
and soul of the one you love

I believe in me
I believe in you
I believe in love
I believe in soul mates
I believe in us
I believe in the promise
Of our life to come

I thank God everyday
I thank God for my family
I thank God for my friends
I thank God for my shelter
I thank God for my full pantry
I thank God for my blessings
I thank God for the most wonderful,
amazing joy of my life
YOU
I thank God for you my darling

How has God blessed me with you
What could I ever have done for you my miracle
I will thank him for the rest of my life
Everyday and everynight
Thank God for blessing me the love of my life

You're the reason I wake up and smile
You're the reason I get out of bed
With a spring in my step
You're the reason I shine
You're the reason I love
You're the reason my heart beats
You're the reason I love life
You're the reason I love me
You're the reason I love

You have the world at your feet
Your essence is layed bare for the world to enjoy
In a sea of heavenly creatures for you to choose
How did I get so lucky that you chose me

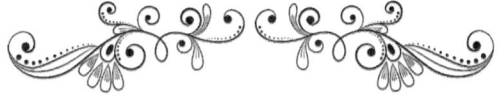

I have been waiting
Waiting days
Waiting weeks
Waiting months
Waiting years
Waiting decades
Waiting for God to send me you
It was worth the wait
I would wait a life time for you

Oh how our nights are filled with pasion
So must our days be filled with love

This journey ahead was scary
before you came into my life
Now the journey ahead is a beacon of shinning light
Waiting for us to enter
Waiting for us to enjoy all that life has to offer
Together we shall walk through this journey
ahead holding hands filled with love

If I fall for you
Will you be there to catch me

How did I wander this earth not knowing
what was missing in my life
How did I walk around blind folded
not seeing what was missing
Now I know that you were missing
How did I survive without you
For I know I could not survive
another day without you

How I long for your lips
To taste you on my tongue
To feel your lips pressed against mine
To get lost in the passion of your kiss
To feel the love of your kiss

I want all of you
The silent you
The distant you
The unsure you
The hurting you
The loving you
The happy you
The joyful you
The blessed you
I want all of you

Let them judge what they do not see
Let them speak of what they do not hear
For our love is solely ours to see and hear

As I lay here
I long for your voice
I long for your touch
I long for your love
I long for your kiss
I long for your body
One day my sweet love
I shall long no more

I love to feel your arms around me
I feel warmth
I feel protected
I feel home
Most of all I feel loved

Your eyes are reflections into your soul
Let me gaze into them
Let me see the stories burried within
Let me be the shoulder of comfort
Let me be the arms of joy
Let me see beyond the surface
Let me touch your soul through your eyes
Your beautiful eyes

Just because we fell in love fast
Don't think it will be as fast to fall out of love
My love is here for a lifetime
I will always be here loving you
Waiting for you
Praying for you
Wishing for you
My love is here forever

It's you as a man
Not who you are to the world
But to me
The real you
In your heart
Your mind
That's the man
I love
That's the only man
I need
That's the man
Who has my heart

You are the one
You are the one I dream about
You are the one I close my eyes and imagine
You are the one I thought I would never find
You are the one I was waiting for
You are the one I found
You are the one
The only one

Perfection
If you look for perfection
You will always be looking
What is perfection to you
To me it's the perfect moon to dance under
The perfect song to sing together
The perfect dinner to make together
The perfect day to make memories
The pefect touch to feel
I love your version of
Perfection

Every day we wake and step into the unknown
How is stepping into the unknown
of your love any different
We don't now what the day has ahead of us
As we don't know what love has in store for us
Get up and take the chance each and everyday

Your arms
Are where I belong
Not for a day
Not for a week
Not for a month
Not for a year
But forever
For in your embrace
Is where I find
My forever

I look to the moon and stars
I see a star burning bright
That star that I make a wish upon
The wish I forever make is for the love of you
I look to the moon and stars
Will my wish come true

As I sit I pour my heart out on paper
Will you ever see this
Will you ever know it is all about you
Will you feel my heart through my words
Will you feel my love pour out on
the pages as you read it
I hope you do
So you know how much I love you

I dream of you
Your words haunt me
Your love comforts me
Your touch excites me
My dreams of you calm me

Though we are oceans apart
I feel your pain
Feel my arms wrap around you to
give you strength and comfort
Close your eyes and feel me as I feel you
I am here for you
Now and always
My darling
Never forget

Well to think you came into my life
With a hello
That's all it took
From there I have lost my heart to you
From there you found my soul

I believe

I believe we will work it out

I believe we are something worth fighting for

I believe we are something worth waiting for

I believe in our love

I believe we will be stronger together

I believe we will end in an all encompassing love

I believe in us

Love sure is a battlefeild
Even if that battlefeild is in my head

Are you real

Am I dreaming

If I am dreaming I never want to wake

I reach out to touch you

I feel your skin on my finger tips

You are real

You are my dream come true

I watch you from afar
I dream of the day when I can touch you
When our two worlds collide
When we can look into each other eyes
When our lips can touch
When I no longer have to watch
When I can close my eyes
And smile

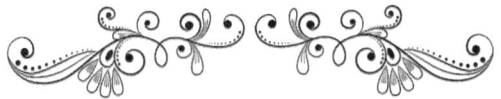

What does it feel like to touch your face
What does it feel like to hear your voice
What does it feel like to dance with you
What does it feel like to hold your hand
What does it feel like to be wrapped in your arms
What does it feel like to kiss your lips
What does it feel like to have you whisper in my ear
What does it feel like to lay my head on
your chest and listen to your heart beat
What does it feel like to lay entwined with you
What does it feel like
I can't wait to find out

Our love is eternal
The flame burns bright
Day and night
It burns through past lives
It will burn forever more
For the flame like ours
Can never be doused

I dream of you
I dream of waking up next to you
I dream of turning over and seeing you next to me
I dream of kissing you good morning
I dream of walking along holding your hand
I dream of laughing together
I dream of making decisions together
I dream of dancing in your arms
I dream of the adventures we will take
I dream of kissing you goodnight
I dream of making love to you
I dream of our love
I dream of our life together
I dream of you

If I close my eyes
I can feel you
I can feel your arms embracing me
I can smell you
Your scent is in the air all around
I can hear you
Your voice that sends my heart into flutter
I just need to keep my eyes closed
Can I keep them closed forever

How I am blessed that you have entered my life
You are a miracle
Miracles are real
You are proof of that
With your words you love me day and night
I have never felt so loved
A love that is all consuming
Consuming my heart and soul to the
depths of the deepest ocean
How can I ever express the love I feel for you
The love that beats strong only for you
A love so pure and bright just like you
Thank you for coming into my life
Thank you for loving me
Thank you for being you
My miracle

I can't get enough of you

Your words

Your smile

Your mind

Your heart

Your soul

Your love

I just can't get enough of you

As I sit and think of you
My emotions overtake me
They bubble to the surface
My tears stream down my face
Tears of utter joy
Tears of utter amazement
What have I ever done to deserve you
I thank God everyday for you
I thank God for bringing me you
You are now my life
You are now my forever

Can you break down my walls
Can you heal my heartbreak
Can you hold my shaking hand
Can you touch my broken soul
Can you trust my words I whisper
Can you trust my heart that now beats for you
Can you trust my lips that touch yours
Can you be the one I have been
Searching my whole life for

I need you to know I'm yours
I need you to know how much you mean to me
I need you to know I love you
I need you to know I worry about you
I need you to know I pray for your safety every day
I need you to know your smile
brings a smile to my face
I need you to know your eyes engulf me
I need you to know I dream of you every night
I need you to know you consume
my every waking hour
I need you to know my days are
better because you are in them
I need you to know I need you
I need you to know my heart beats for you
I need you to know I am yours, mind, body and soul

I want you to feel
Loved all the time
I want you to always
Have a beautiful smile on your face
Your heart to always feel full
With my love for you

I stand and wait for you
Wait amongst everyone waiting for their loved ones
I've been waiting a life time for
you to come into my life
I see you
Your beautiful smile
Your beautiful eyes
I'm overcome with joy
I'm overcome with the love I feel for you
We embrace
Our love flows into each other
Our lips meet for the first time
Not for the last time
But the begining of a lifetime

How have you walked into my life
Like you belong there
Like you have always been there
Like you are needed there
Like you will never leave
Like your heart is mine forever

I hope you feel how much I love you
I hope my words convey how much you mean to me
I hope my love flows into your heart
I hope you see how much you have changed my life
I hope you feel how much I love you
I hope you feel how much I need you
Not to save me
But to love me
To love me the way I love you
A love that is eternal
A love only for you

Shall we dance under the moonlight
Shall we kiss under the moonlight
Shall we make love under the moonlight
Shall we proclaim our everlasting
love under the moonlight
Only the moonlight shall know
Only the moonlight shall hold our secrets
Only the moonlight shall know of our love

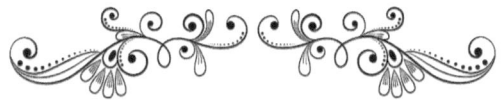

Love

It feels so wonderful when you hear I love you

It feels so amazing to say I love you

Love is such a powerful drug

Love is all you need to feel cherished

It feels like floating in the air when you feel loved

It feels like your life is complete when you feel loved

Love is such a roller coaster

Love is such a need from within

It feels like nothing can stop you

It feels like the world is yours

Love is all around you

Love is yours to let in

It feels like your life has just begun

It feels like you can conquer the world

Love is beautiful

Love is how I feel about you

You have stormed into my life like a tornado of love
I thought I had battened down
the hatches of my heart
But you came along and blew them off
You have opened my heart after the storm
My heart has been repaired better than ever
You have mended my broken heart
with your tornado of love

I love you

1 4 3

3 words

Just 8 letters

On their own

I, such a selfish word

Love, a word of endless possibilities

You, a word that can be so descriptive

Put them all together

I love you is so powerful

Power to provoke happiness

Power to provoke a smile

Power to provoke dreaming

Power to change someone's life

Power to change someones world

Power to change your own world forever

3 of the most powerful words you can say

Only to be used with meaning

Only to be used when your heart is full

Only to be used for one amazing person

I love You

How can you be real
You are a dream come true
You make me cry tears of joy
If this is a dream
I hope I never wake

When I think of my life I think of you
When I think of comfort I think of you
When I think of happiness I think of you
When I think of joy I think of you
When I think of safety I think of you
When I think of love I think of you
When I think of the future I think of you
When I think of forever I think of you

I have been waiting for love to come my way
Waiting year after year
Longing for love
Waiting for the love you read about
Longing for my heart to beat for another
Waiting for the day I could love another
Longing for my soulmate to come along
Waiting for you

Oh how my heart longs for you
It longs to beat next to you
Day and night
When you are not with me it longs for you
I wake and it longs for you
I go about my day longing for you
I lay down to sleep aching or you
I dream of the day I no longer spend
my days and night longing for you
The day my heart will beat next to yours
The day my heart never has to ache for you again
The day you feel my love beating next to you
Beating only for you

My heart feels so full of love
Love for you
It beats fast whenever I think of you
It beats fast whenever we talk
It beats a love of a life time
Love that feels so right
Love I have never felt before
A beat that will go on forever

You came into my life and changed it forever
That was the best day of my life
You make everyday feel like a blessing
Thank you for the gift of love
you have bestowed on me
My love for you is immeasurable
I feel words can not express the love
I feel for you in my heart
I thank God everyday for bringing you into my life
I have cried many tears over the years
I have never cried so many sweet
tears since I met you
My tears for you are tears of joy
I can't wait to spend the rest of my life with you
You are my Angel
Sent from above

You are as rich as big as your heart
As opening your heart to others
Makes you rich with love

You have engulfed every sleeping
and waking moment
I can't imagine my life without you in it
I can't imagine you not in it even for a minute
How have I lived this life without you in it
How I now realise my life was so empty
Empty of love
Empty because you were not in it
My heart beats only for you

I have been waiting
Waiting for a love I thought would never come
I never thought I could meet the most amazing man
A man who has awakened my heart and soul
A soul that has been searching
Searching for it's other half
The wait is over

I go outside
I look up at the sky
What a beautiful sight
I close my eyes
I make a wish
I wish for a love
A love so true
A love so beautiful
A love that's here to stay
A love that lasts a life time
I make a wish upon a star
I make a wish
For you

I want to roll over and see your face
I want to roll over and kiss your lips
I want to roll over and whisper into your ear
I want to roll over and be wrapped in your arms
I want to roll over and love you
I want to roll over and make love to you
I want to roll over and be loved by you

You want me to write about you
About my love for you
Maybe
About your engulfing eyes
About your beautiful smile
Your soulful voice
Your intelligent mind
Your warm heart
Your deep soul
Why do I love you
I just do

Where ever you are is where I want to be
I will follow you to where ever you want to go
Qatar, Milan, London, Japan anywhere
Where ever you are is my home
I will follow you to the moon and back
if that is where you want to be
Just know I'll be there for you
Loving you
Always

Why do I love you
How can I put what I'm feeling into words
How do I explain this need to talk to you
How do I explain this need to see you
How do I explain this need to touch you
How do I explain this need to be in your arms
How do I explain this need to kiss you
How do I explain the ache in my
heart when I'm not with you
How do I explain the emptiness without you
Why do I love you
I just do

If your lucky
Someone will come into your world
Who will turn your life around
Show you what it's like to be truly loved
A love so deep and pure
A love you thought never really
excisted only in fairy tales
A love that you never want to live without

When I look up at night
I see the stars
Shinning so brightly
Shinning like magic
Shinning
Waiting for me to make a wish
I close my eyes
I make my wish
I open my eyes
There you are
My wish
Shinning like the star you are

Your arms that's where I belong
Wrapped in your love
Feeling safe
Feeling comfort
Feeling protected
Feeling peace
Feeling like I never want to leave

As I sit here and think of you
My mind wonders how you have entered my heart
My heart was once broken into many pieces
I didn't know if the pieces would
ever fit back together
I thought I would of had to stomp them back in
you have gently placed them back together
My heart has been loveingly repaired
Thank you for your love
That has mended my fallen pieces

I finally found someone
Someone who makes my life complete
Someone to walk with me through lifes journeys
Someone to take adventures with
Someone who makes me want to be a better person
Someone who has touched my heart
in ways I never new possible
Someone to spend the rest of my life with
Someone to call home

Even though we have never met
I know you are the one for me
You are my soul mate
You are the love of my life
My forever
One day we will meet
One day the universe will bring us together
One day we will look into each
others eyes and know
I will wander this earth to find you
We will meet and know we are meant to be
Meant to be together forever
The one I have been looking for
The only one
The last one
One day

Any where you are is home
Home is where my heart is
My heart is with you
You are the one I love
The one I love today, tomorrow and forever

I believe in destiny
I believe you and I were meant to be
I believe that everything happens for a reason
I believe you have been sent from God
I believe you are my soul mate
I believe you are the love of my life
I believe you are my destiny
I believe you love me
Believe I love you

Your voice was music to my ears
I have dreamt of what your voice would sound like
My dreams never came close to
your beautiful melody
Thank you for the gift of your voice
A voice that makes my heart race
A voice that promises love
A voice that captures your essance
The magic of your voice

I wan't to be that couple
That couple people talk about
That couple people want to emulate
That couple people watch in movies
That couple people read about in books
That couple people dream of being a part of
That couple who hold hands walking down the street
That couple who smile at each other
just because they see at each other
That couple who kiss and don't care who is watching
That couple who are always there for each other
That couple who call during the
day just to hear your voice
That couple who never want to
be away from each other
I just want to be that couple
With you

Do you believe in fate
Do you believe we have been brought together by fate
Fated to love
Fated to learn
Fated to be together
Fated to bring our hearts together
Fated to bring our souls to aline
Fate knew what we needed
We needed each other

I'm walking down the street
I'm looking around
I'm looking for you
I'm looking for your smile
I'm looking for your eyes
I'm looking for your soul
I don't know you
Yet I'm looking for you
For you are my soul mate
For you are my other half
I'm looking for you
Where are you

Let the light shine upon us
Shine upon our love
Shine upon our hearts
Shine upon our souls
Shine the light upon our wishes
Shine the light upon our dreams
Shine the light upon our future
Shine the light upon us
Shine upon
Me and you

I look outside
The clouds are thick and heavy
I look outside
The rain is falling
I look outside
Rain is sliding down the windows
I look outside
I can't see
I look outside
My eyes are blurry
I look outside
My tears stream down my face
I look outside
I can't stop crying
I look outside
I can't see you
I look outside
The rain has stopped
I look outside
I see a rainbow
I look outside
I can see clearly again
I look outside
I know I'll find love again
I look outside
I can smile again
I look outside
I can't wait to live life again
As I look outside

It's got to be you

No one else can compare to your love

No one else can love me the way you do

No one else will ever kiss me the way you do

No one else can hold me the way you do

No one else will ever hold my heart in their hand

No one else will ever know my soul the way you do

So it's got to be you

Only you

I see your words
My eyes excite me
I want to hear your voice
So my heart can hear you
I want to talk to you
So you can hear my heart
Not just see it in words
But hear it in my words
I want to hear your heart
Through your voice
Let me hear your heart
Let me hear your voice

My love
The distance is great
Our love is near
Distance has not hampered our love
Our love is strong
Strong enough to last the distance and time
True love conquers all
Never doubt my love
My love is forever and true

I see you
You are beautiful
You smile
I smile back
You stop
I'm surprised
You say hello
I return the hello
You ask to have a coffee
I'm surprised
But I agree
What will the coffee bring
I hope coffee leads to us
A future us
We smile

I want a love that is pure
I want a love that lasts a life time
I want a love that is easy
I want a love that isn't vengeful
I want a love that isn't hard
I want a love that makes me smile
I want a love that makes my heart sore
I want a love that makes me dream
I want a love that lasts forever

You came into my life
Like a whirlpool
You captured my heart
You captured my soul
You gave me a glimpse of the future
You gave me a piece of your heart
I gave you my heart
I gave you my mind
I gave you my body
I gave you my love
As you wrapped me
In your whirlpool of love
That captured me

I open my eyes
My first thought is of you
I look at my phone
I smile
Your morning message is there to greet me
What a fabulous way to start the day
Your message makes my heart beat faster
My life is better because your in it

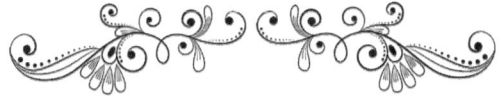

Heart beat
I can feel your heart beat
Your golden heart beat
Beating in your chest
Beating for me
Beating strong for our love
Your golden heart beat
I lay my head against your chest
And listen to your golden heart beat
Beating stronger and stronger
Your Heart beat

You envelope me from behind
You whisper you love me in my ear
I turn my head
You kiss my lips
I turn around in your arms
I know I'm home
I never want to leave

Do you ever dream of an all consuming love
Do you ever think you will find that love
Do you even think that, that kind of love exists
Do you think it will find you soon
Do you think you will have to travel far to find it
Do you think you deserve that kind of love
Do you think that love deserves you
YES, YES,YES,YES,YES
Yes to all of it
You do

I look into your eyes
I dream of them
I touch your lips
I melt into them
I touch your face
I never want to stop
I touch your body
I never want to let go

Nothing is going to change my love
My love is here to stay
There is nothing you can say or do
To change my love for you
I will be here in good times
I will be here in bad times
I will be here for you always
I'll be here today, tomorrow and forever
For there is nothing
That can change this love
I have for you

I love your smile
Your smile lights up your face
Your smile makes my heart race
Your smile shows a beautiful soul within
I love to see your smile just for me

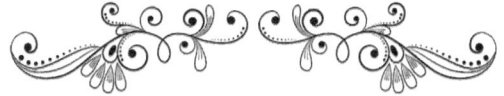

I love the way you look at me
Like I'm the only one alive
I love the way you smile at me
Like I'm eveything you have wished for
I love the way you touch me
Like I am so precious I may break
I love the way you love me
Like I'm every dream come true

With every drop of rain
With every ray of sun
With every glow of the moon
Your golden heart shines through
Shines through every glistening drop of rain
Shines through every golden ray of the sun
Shines through every sparkling glow of the moon
Your golden heart shines through

I look over at you
You are looking at me
Your look starts my engine
I want to start yours
Your engine that will ignite my love
My love that will never die
My love that will smoulder for years to come
You have the key to my heart
I want to start your engine with my key
I want the key to your heart to never turn off
But to idle day and night

How do the stars shine from your eyes
It looks like God took the stars from the sky
and gave them to you
For your eyes to shine for everyone to see
Shinning brightly like sparkling diamonds
Oh how do the stars shine from your eyes

When she is done
You will know
She is not here to play games
She is not here to be your mother
She is not here for your entertainment
She is not here for a day
She is not here for a week
She is not here for a month
She is looking for her forever
Are you looking for your forever

Do you believe in love
Do you believe in soul mates
Do you believe in twin flames
Do you believe in forever

Let me lay my head against your chest
Let me hear the beat of your heart
Let me hear the love beating within
Tell me the story burried within
Let me hear the story
Let me feel the story
Let me hear your heart beat
As I lay my head against your chest
I want to hear it all

You're on my mind
You're in my heart
You're deep within my soul
You're burried into my core
You are apart of me

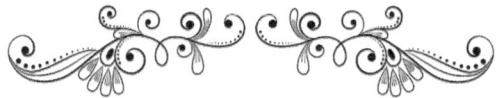

Put your hand in mine
Let me lead you through this journey
This journey we call life
This jouney which is a maze
The maze of love
Follow me through the maze
Follow me to the end
To the end of our lives
Put your hand in mine

If I had you in my life
The science of love
Would be to find out how your heart beats
What makes your heart beat to the rhythm of love
The rhythm deep within your soul
Deep within your heart
Beating day and night
Show me the science of your love
That beats so bright

Have you
Ever felt
A love so great
A love like no other
True unconditional love
You can't go a day without them
You feel like you can't breath without them
You feel like life is not worth living without them
You feel your heart beats faster just thinking of them
You feel a happiness so great for
them being in your life
You feel you don't even have the
words to explain your love
Have you ever felt that all encompassing
all consumming type of love
If you have felt that type of love you are
one of the few lucky ones in life

It dosen't matter how many minutes tick
It dosen't matter how many hours pass
It dosen't matter how many weeks go by
It dosen't matter how many months turn over
It dosen't matter how many years roll on
No amount of time
Is going to change my love for you

Smile for you are alive
Smile for you are blessed
Smile for you are living life
Smile for the sun is shinning
Smile for the flowers are blooming
Smile for the stars are twinkling
Smile for the moon is beaming
Smile for you are loved
Smile for you can love
Smile for you can embrace the world
Smile for life is a chance to fulfill your dreams
Smile everyday because you can

It's you
It has always been you
It will always be you
No one else can compare
No one else will ever come close
To you
It's you
Only You

Blessings

What is a blessing

A blessing is waking up each day

A blessing is having food to eat

A blessing is having clothes to wear

A blessing is having friends that love you

A blessing is having a friend to love

A blessing is having family that love you

A blessing is having family to love

A blessing is having someone in your life

A blessing is having someone to love

A blessing is having someone love you

My biggest blessing is you

My heart is full
Full of love
Full of love for you
Full for evermore

Are you ready
Are you ready for us
Are you ready for this love
Are you ready for this journey together
Are you ready for a life time of us
Are you ready for forever
Tell me
Are you ready

Put your hand in mine
Lets walk through this journey together
Together we shall explore this life
Hand in hand
Together as one
Together along the path to happiness

You took the words out of my mouth
3 little words
3 little words with so much impact
3 little words I wanted to tell you
3 little words I feel for you
3 little words that mean so much
3 little words I love to hear
3 little words my heart needs to say
3 little words
I love you

We have the time
We have the laughs
We have the words
We have the actions
We have the love
We have the heart
We have the soul
We have the always
We have forever

I love having conversations with you
I love how you make me laugh
I love how you get my jokes
I love how you get my life
I love how you care about me
I love how you make plans
I love how we can talk for hours
I love how you support my dreams
I love how you make me feel whole
I love how the world with you makes sense
I just love you, all of you

You make my heart smile
When you make my heart sing
I can't stop smiling
I can't stop singing
My heart is about to explode
With the thoughts of you

If you plant the seeds of love
They will grow into a love so great
A love only you can nurture
A love you need to water
A love you need to feed
A love you need to take care of
A love you can watch grow
A love you will be proud of
A love only to be found in your garden
For you have watched this grow
From seeds to maturity
A love only for you

I hope this finds you
Finds you happy
Finds you smiling
Finds you loving yourself
Finds you being loved
Finds you having someone to love
Finds you living your best life
I hope this finds you living your dreams

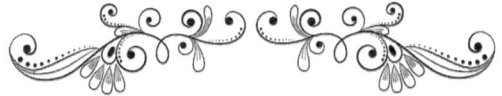

Life is like being on a ferris wheel
You can't wait to ride it
Once your on it, it's fun
But after awhile
It just keeps going in circles
Around and around
Then you just want it to stop
Sometimes you even want to get off
You need to find someone
Someone to take that ride with you
Someone to make the ride fun again
Soemone you want to go around with
Around and around
Find someone to ride that ferris wheeel with

I'm on my way to you
I'm on my way to us
I've been travelling this journey of life
I've been travelling this road to you
Wait for me to get to you
Keep your heart open for me
Keep your faith in us
Please wait for us
I'm on my way to your love

I'm on my way
On my way to hug you
On my way to be with you
On my way kiss you
On my way be held in your arms
On my way to lay with you
On my way to sitting and talking together
On my way to cook together
On my way to walk along holding hands
On my way to dance under the stars
On my way to love you
Darling I'm on my way

I always get what I want
What I want is you

Stolen moments
Stolen moments of time
Stolen moments of laughter
Stolen moments together
Stolen moments of kisses
Stolen moments of smiles
Stolen moments of hugs
Stolen moments of love
Enjoy the stolen moments

My eyes are blue like saphires
My heart is red like rubies
My soul is pure white like pearls
But you are my diamond
You are the most precious stone of all

The way you look at me
Makes my smile beam
Makes my heart beat faster
Makes my soul melt
Makes me happier than you could imagine
Makes me glad to be alive
Only you
Could look at me like that

Memories of you
Memories of us
Memories of yesterday
Memories of tomorrow to come
Memories of our love
Memories forever to last a lifetime
I love my memories

You don't choose who you love
Your heart chooses
Your heart chooses who it beats for
Your heart chooses who it bleeds for
Your heart chooses who it breaks for
Your heart has the only choice
Your heart loves who it wants
Your heart is your only chance
Only chance for love
Let your heart choose

The flames burns brightly
Burns day and night
Burns for your love
Burns for you
Flickering
Burning
Only for you
Evermore

No one makes me happy
The way you do
Just standing next to you
With your arms
Around me
Everyday is like a new day
I never want you to let go
I never want this moment to end
I feel like I'm living in a dream
Everyday with you in it

As long as you love me
My days will be amazing
My nights will be extraodinary
Today is remarkable
Tomorrow will be breathtaking
As long as you love me

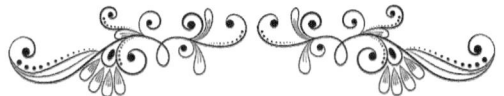

I count the days
The days to we will be together
The days until I can kiss your lips
The days until I can be in your arms
The days until we no longer have to say
Goodbye
The days that will turn into nights
The days that will last forever
I count the days

You are my gift
You are the only gift I want
The only gift I'll ever need
The only gift
No gift will ever compare to you
No gift is as precious as you

There's no limit on our love
I love you unconditionally
A love that knows no end
There is no limit on our hearts
My heart is yours always
Two hearts beating as one
There is no limit on our souls
My soul is forever yours
Two souls forever intwined

Your touch ignites me
Your lips burn againt my skin
Your love explodes in my heart
My soul feels like it is going to burst into flames
Just from that one touch

I'm diving right in
Diving into your eyes
Diving into your arms
Diving into your lips
Diving into your heart
Diving into your soul
Diving into your love
Diving into you

I want to dance the night away with you
I want to dance under the stars
I want to dance in the moonlight
I want to dance in your arms
I want to dance with you forever
Where ever that dance takes us

I'm carving my way to you
Carving through the wall I have built
Carving through the pain I have felt
Carving through the worry I feel
Carving through the barrier I have put up
Carving through my broken heart
Carving through my bleeding soul
Can you wait
While I carve through to you

I always new you were meant for me
I feel it in my heart
I feel it in my soul
I feel it in every breath I take
I feel it down to my core
You were meant for me
I was meant for you

I tell myself
I must be dreaming
I tell myself
This can't be happening
I tell myself
I must be imagining this
I tell myself
This is not real
I tell myself
All of this
But yet here we are
Living in my dreams
Living the love of a life time

You said it first
I didn't get the chance
To tell you
I love you
You said it first
But I'll say it last
I love you

I cross my heart
When I say I love you
I cross my heart
When I say you hold my heart
In your hand
I cross my heart
When I say my soul
Is yours too keep
I cross my heart
When I say I promise
To love you
Forever

You are my angel
I want to be in your arms
In the arms of my angel
Don't let me go
Hold me tight
Hold me forever
My angel

Love is love
Love is there for us to find
To find with a soul mate
Love is something to be valued
Love is to be cherished
Love is to be appreciated
Appreciate finding that one
The one you can feel comfort
The one you can feel safe
The one you can feel joy
The one who feels like home
Love is Love

Your the only one for me
The only one I want
The only one my heart wants
The only one my soul wants
The only one for me

You are the kryptonite to my heart
My heart was solid
My heart was strong
My heart was secure
My heart was powerful
My heart was indestructible
Until you came along
You broke down my heart
You are the kryptonite to my heart

I'm scared to tell you
Tell you how I feel
To tell you how deep Im feeling for you
To tell you I love you
I'm scared to tell you
In case you don't feel it too

Your the only one
The only one who has my heart
The only one with the key to my heart
My heart is yours
Please look after it
Please don't break it
Please treat it with love
I don't want anyone else to have it
Only you have my heart

A love like ours
Is hard to find
For it is heaven sent
Sent from above
Sent to last a life time

My heart sings for you
Sings day and night
Singing strong
Singing loud
Singing like a karaoke machine
Of love songs
It never stops singing
Singing for you

I've nailed it
Nailed my love for you
Nailed my heart to yours
Nailed our hearts together
Nailed our souls to hold forever
Strong as nails
Nailed together

When you love someone
The little things don't matter
The big things are there
To get through together
To make you stronger
When you love someone
You see what no one else sees
You see the beauty within
You see into their heart
You see into their soul
When you love someone

I finally found the one
I finally found the love of my life
I finally found my soul mate
I finally found my forever

I've got you
Nothing else matters
The rain can beat down
The sun can set
The clouds can darken the skies
The stars can hide
Nothing matters
As long as I've got you

If you love someone
Tell them
Life is too short for rergrets

I love to hear the rain beating down
Beating above us
Lying in bed smiling
You, holding me in your arms
Is the only place I want to be
If I died right now
Nothing could compare
As I am already in heaven

Who can say why I care
Who can say why I love you
Who can say how our love grows
Who can say how long our love will last
Who can say how long the distanst will measure
Who can say how long forever will be
And in he end
Does it really matter
As long as there is love

If this is it
If this is what love is
I am the happiest person on earth
If I died tomorrow I could say I did it
I found true love
I found the person I would die for
The person who has made my dreams come true
The person who is my world
I did it
I found the love of my life
I found my true love

I have loved you every day
I have loved you every night
I have loved you every minute
I have loved you every hour
I have loved you in my heart
I have loved you in my soul
I can not see myself
But love you forever

Wrapped up in your arms
Is where I want to be
I want to be wrapped in them
Forever
I want to never leave
For in your arms is where I find love
Where I find comfort
Where I find strength
Where I find happiness
Wrapped up in your arms

My love is true

My love is yours

My love is worn on my sleeve

My love is bared for all to see

My love is for today

My love is for tomorrow

My love is forever

My love is yours

My love is true

Shall we walk through the fields of flowers
With the sun shining through the trees
Radiating on our faces as we walk
Hand in hand along the path
Shall we crunch through the amber leaves
As the wind wisps across our skin
As we walk arm in arm along
The trail through whispering trees
Shall we sink into the snow covered ground
Chilling our bodies as we make
Snow angels in the fresh flakes
Finger tip to finger tip in the crisp air
Shall we run through the bulbs of daffodils
Scenting the aura with their sweet perfume
That floats through the breeze
As we stroll hands intwind along the avenue

In case you don't know
The way I feel about you
The way my heart melts
The way my soul shines
The way mind dreams
The way my body races
In case you didn't know
I just wanted to tell you
I love you

You are the moon
I am the sun
You are the day
I am the night
You are the yin
To my yang
You are meant for me
I was meant for you
You are the last piece of my puzzle
I never new was missing
We will fit together forever
Finally finding the soul
That completes mine

Every time I look into your eyes
I want to tell you how I feel
I want to tell you I drown in your eyes
I want to tell you I feel I can see into your soul
I want to tell you my heart melts
every time you look at me
Every time I look into your eyes
I want to tell you
I love you

I'm giving you my heart
Please be gentle with it
As it is fragile
From all the heartbreak
From all the broken promises
But it needs to feel love again
So I'm giving it to you
To love
Like I know only you can
For your gentle ways
Your gentle words
I know my heart
Will be forever safe
In your loving hands

I'm blinded by your love
I can't see a life without you in it
I can't imagine you not next to me
I can't see my future without you
I can't imagine my nights without you
I can't see spending my days without you
I can't imagine spending a minute away from you
I wouldn't want it any other way
Then being blinded by your love

I close my eyes
I see you
I close my eyes
I feel you
I close my eyes
My heart aches for you
I close my eyes
My souls yearns for you
I close my eyes
The distance dissapates
I close my eyes
You are here with me
I close my eyes
I am dreaming
Dreaming of a time and place
Where we can never be apart

You have awakened my heart
You have awakened my soul
You have awakened my mind
That there is truly unconditinal love
Unconditional love between two people
Unconditional love that can be trusted
Unconditional love that will last a life time
You have awakened me to believe in love again

You are never alone
For I am here for you
Here for you every minute of the day
Here for you every minute of the night
Here for you day and night
You will never be alone
I will be always here for you
Never doubt that
Never doubt my love
My love for you
Is here to stay
You will never be alone again

Like a bird drawn to heaven
Is how you draw me to you
For the pull of your love
Is intoxicating
Is irresistable
Is inticing
I'm drawn to your love
Like a bird drawn to the heavens

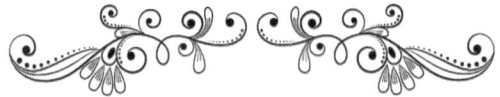

In this big world
I feel small
I am but 1
Looking for you
Looking for you to make the world
Seem not so big
Not so alone
Not so small
Where are you
In this big world
1 looking for 2

Flying high
On the wings of an angel
That's what love feels like
That's what loving you feels like
Flying high on the wings of an angel

I know you are out there waiting for me
Waiting for me to find you
I'm on my way
On my way to find you
On my way to your waiting arms
On my way to your waiting love
I'm on my way
To your love

Can we measure the depth of our love
How deep is your love
How deep is my love
Only our hearts shall measure
Only our souls shall know

As I sit and wonder
I wonder how long you will love me
I wonder how long will I love you
I wonder how long will this moment last
I wonder how long will this love last
As I sit and wonder
I shall wonder no more
For I know this love is here to stay
This love is forever

Time stands still
Whenever you're around
My heart beats faster
But time beats slower
I don't want this moment to ever end
I want time to stand still forever

Im falling for you
Falling for your smile
Falling for your laughter
Falling for your mind
Falling for your heart
Falling for your soul
Im falling for you
Falling for every part of you
Forever falling
In love with you

Put your hand in mine
Let me lead the way
Lead the way to happiness
Lead the way to love
Lead the way to the future
Lead the way to forever

I knew one day I would find you
I knew you were out there waiting for me
Waiting for a love to come and change your world
Waiting for a love to come and change my world
I knew that one day if I waited long enough
I would find you
We would find each other
I just had to have faith
That one day I would find you

You were meant for me
You were the one
The one God made for me

You are everything
Everything I have dreamt of
Everything I could of imagined
You are beautiful
Beautiful inside and out
You are amazing
Just as you are

My arms are empty without you
I want to feel you in them again
For my arms are where you belong
My life is where you belong
My love is where you belong
My heart is where you belong
We belong together
Wrapped in each others arms

My heart is empty
There is a space that needs filling
It's waiting for a pure love
A love that does not have to wonder
A love that knows no heart break
A love that wants to give joy
A love that wants to give happiness
A love that wants to protect
A love that wants to share
A love that knows how to give and take
My heart is waiting for your love

I'm on my way
On my way to your love
On my way to happiness
On my way to my future
My future that shines bright
Shines for all the world to see
My world with you
For you are my world
I'm on my way
My love

My lifes journey has led me to you
For all the ups and all the downs
Life has given me
Has led me to this moment
This moment in time
This moment when you have entered my life
You have entered my life with a
love I never new possible
A love that one could only dream about
A love that I am ready for
A love I am ready to give
For life has brought me through to you
To love and be loved
For a life time of heartbreak
Has lead to a lifetime of love
With you

It's rough out there
It's hard to find the one
There are so many rough cuts
I am looking for a diamond
Looking for a diamond in the rough

Heaven sent me you
Sent you to heal my heart
Sent you to show me love
Sent you to show me happiness
Sent you to give me life again
Sent you to give me hope
Sent you to be wrapped in your love
Sent you to see the future
Sent you to beleive in miracles
You are truly Heaven sent

You feel like home
My heart knows you
My soul feels you
Wherever you are is my home
For when I'm near you it feels right
When you are gone I feel empty
It doesn't matter where you are
That's home to me

I once wrote about nothing

Feeling nothing

Having a heart so hurt

There was nothing inside

Once again I'm writting about nothing

Though in feeling so much

Now having a heart so full

There is so much inside

I can not put what I'm feeling

Into words

For there are no words

In the world

To convay the love I feel for you

So once again I'm writting about nothing

You make me happy every day
With all the things you do
For you make every day filled with joy
Every day filled with love
Every day filled with wonderment
Every day is a blessing to have you in it

The river is flowing
Just like my mind is flowing
With thoughts of you
The sun is shinning
Just like my heart is shinning
With warmth for you
The birds are singing
Just like my soul is singing
With love for you

You touched my heart like no one has ever done
I didn't know a love like this existed until I met you
For you have awakened my heart to what real love is
A love I now know exists
Not only in books and movies
But in a world of beauty filled with love

Can you feel it coming
You know it's coming
You just have to be patient
For you know in your heart
That love is coming for you
You deserve unconditional love
Your person is on the way
Smile and keep on being you
For you know it won't be long now

You are my knight in shinning armour
You have ridden in and swooped me up
Into your loving arms
Arms that promise to love me
Arms that promise to protect me
Arms that promise forever

I want to be with you everyday
I want to be with you every night
Wherever you are is home to me
My heart belongs to you
So take my heart where ever you need to go
As I will follow you day and night
Where ever you go I will be there
Waiting and loving forever

Love is kind
Love is caring
Love is patient
Love is thoughtful
Love is seeing the best in someone
Love is looking for the good in everyone

You have healed my heart
My heart that thought it could never love another
Then you entered my life and
entered my heart with love
You showed me everyday
Just what love could do
How did I get so lucky

What is the colour of love
Some say red
For the heart is red
Some say white
White for a pure love
What about black
Black like some souls
What colour is love
What colour is your love

I have written about love
I have written about loss
I have written about joy
I have written about sorrow
I have written about me
I have written about us
Have I found the answer
Have I found the meaning of love
Have I got any idea what happens next
I just know I can't give you up
For our love is unconditional
For our love will be in my soul forever
I will continue writing about love
For I have not written everything
About us
To come

If you do it with love
It's never wrong

My mind yearns for you
My body aches for you
My eyes cry for you
My heart bleeds for you
My soul searches for you

You are my light
You are my sunshine
You are the moon glistening
You are the stars sparkling above
You are the reason I shine so bright
Day and night

You look over at me
My heart melts
You smile
My heart misses a beat
You blow me a kiss
My heart explodes
You come over
My heart races
You touch my face
My heart stops beating

I don't want yesterdays
I don't want anymore todays
I just want a whole life time of tomorrows
With you

Can you feel the warmth of the sun
Shinning down upon us
I lift my face towards the rays
I feel the rays glistening upon my face
I feel so warm
I feel so blessed
I feel so joyous
To feel the sun
Bestowing it's warmth upon us

From dusk till dawn
From Dawn till dusk
Not a minute of the day
Nor a mintute of the night
Goes by that I don't love you
More than yesterday

Don't give up
Don't give up on love
Can you feel it
Feel it coming for you
So don't give up now
Don't miss what's coming for you
Don't miss what's meant for you
All those lessons
Were there to make you
The best version of you
Don't waste them
For the best is yet to come

If you love some one
Tell them
Don't have regrets
Of what might have been

You comfort me with your words
You comfort me with your arms
Your comfort me with every beat of your heart
You comfort me with your love
I feel comfort just thinking of you
I feel comfort just looking at you
You are my comfort
You are my world

You are my happiness
You are my future
Take my hand
Lets travel this life together
Hand in hand

In a world filled with so many
How have we found each other
How have we managed to find
The one person who completes us
The one person who loves us
Unconditionally
How have we managed to find
That one true love

If you are ever lucky enough
To find the one
Hold on tight and never let go

Just keep loving me the way you do
For no one has ever loved me like you do
With such conviction
With such love
With such passion
Don't ever stop
Loving me the way you do

You are my ying to my yang
We just fit together
We were made for each other
Made for this life time
Made for many life times

As we walk along the path
Our hands softly brush together
You gently take my hand in yours
I feel the love as our hands entwine
I feel the passion we share
I feel the love flow between us
As we walk along the path

I want to kiss you
I want to taste your lips
I want to feel your lips
Pressed against mine
I want to kiss you
Until we think of nothing else
Except that feeling of magic
Of your lips against mine

I want you to fall in love with me
Fall in love with my mind
Fall in love with my eyes
Fall in love with my sense of humour
Fall in love with my heart
Fall in love with my soul
I want you to fall in love with me
The real me
The me that matters
The me that lasts
The me that will be there a life time

I want to lay in your arms
I want to lay there forever
Wrapped in your embrace
Feeling safe
Feeling loved
Laying in your arms

True love is beautiful
True love is powerful
True love makes the heart beat faster
True love makes you smile
True love makes you feel you have wings
To fly
True loves makes you feel you
can conquor the world
True love is something we all search for

Thoughts of you
Are forever woven in my mind
The feel of you
Forever felt on my skin
The taste of you
Forever glistening on my lips
The sound of your voice
Forever whispering in ears
The sight of you
Forever dancing in my eyes
The love for you
Forever embedded in my heart

Every day I think of you
You are always on my mind
Why can I not stop thinking of you
Just one day of not having you on my mind
What would that be like
I don't know
For you have been on my mind
Everyday for such a long time
I wouldn't know what else would be
occupying my mind
I wouldn't know what that feels like
Not to have you with me every day
Always on my mind

The love we share
Can not be mearsured
For it is immeasurable
The love we share
It can not be timed
For it is timeless
The love we share
Can not be spoken about
For there are no words compare
The love we share
Is immeasurable, timeless and imcomparable

I want you to love me
The way I love you
I want to see into your soul
I want to know every part of you
I want to read your mind
I want you when you are happy
I want you when you are sad
I want you when you feel exilerated
I want you when you are a mess
I want to be the one you share
your achievements with
I want to be the one to comfort
you in times of sorrow
I want you every day
I want you forever
I to be your one

Your smile is beautiful
I love your smile
It touches my heart
I could watch you smile forever

I have been waiting for you
Waiting for you to come into my life
Come in and never leave
For you have captured my heart
I never want you to give it back
Keep it safe
Cherish it
Love it

Love makes a garden grow
Watching the blooms stand tall
With the watering of love you give
Water each day with love
Watch how the one you love
Blooms from the love you give

Your are my dream come true
I could never of imagined having you in my life
In my wildest dreams I wished for you
Thinking you would never be real
Thinking I was only dreaming
You make me happy
You make my heart sing
You make my soul shine
You are my dream come true

You are out there somewhere
I don't know where you are
I don't know who you are
I just know
You are out there
Waiting for me to find you
Waiting for me to love you

I see you walking down the path
Your smile is infectious
I can't help but smile back
I get excited just seeing you
Knowing you are walking to me
Walking to our life ahead
For the life ahead is filled with blessings
Days filled with laughter
Nights filled with love
I can't stop smiling
Watching you walking down the path

You're the only one
The only one who has my heart
The only one with the key to my heart
My heart is yours
Please look after it
Please don't break it
Please treat it with love
I don't want anyone else to have it
Only you have my heart

Nothing smells better than freshly picked flowers
Nothing smells better than fresh falling rain
Nothing smells better than you after a shower
Nothing feels better than the sun
beating on your face
Nothing feels better than a kiss on your lips
Nothing feels better than you lying next to me
Nothing looks better than petals after the rain
Nothing looks better than waves washing over sand
Nothing looks better on you than me
Nothing is better than you with me

My world was grey
Sometimes black
Sometimes white
Now my world is filled with many colours
Colours you have put there
Colours that have changed my life
For you are the colour
That has changed my world

You are the air I breathe
You are the water I need
You are the river that flows
You are the sun that shines
You are the stars that sparkle
You are the moon that glows
You are the one that makes the days brighter
You are the one who makes the nights forever
You are the one I need
Who makes my life complete

I just want to feel your hand in mine
I just want to feel your breath on my neck
I just want to feel your arms wrapped around me
I just want to feel your lips on mine
I just want to feel your body touching mine
I just want to feel your love in my heart
I just want to feel your soul entering mine

You are like water to me
I need you to survive
I can't go on for many days without you
I need to have you in my life
For you are like water that flows
Through my viens
Keeping me alive
Keeping my heart pumping
Keeping my soul beating

Love will wait a life time
Just to see you face to face
Just for a chance of that kiss
Just for a chance of something more
For a love that is true
There is no time limit

When I see you coming towards me
I can't stop smiling
The dreams start to form
The life ahead seems brighter
My body starts to shake
You make it hard to breathe
You make my heart beat out of my chest
Nothing elese matters
The world stops spinning
When I see you coming towards me

Every time you think of me
You send a sign
A sign in my day
A sign in my mind
A sign in my dreams
I know every time you are thinking of me
I feel you
Because you send a sign

If you love someone
You want to tell the world
You want to shout from the rooftops
If you love someone
Nothing is ever to much
You will do anything for them
If you love someone
You can't stop smilimg
You can't stop laughing
If you love someone
Your heart races
Your soul sings
If you love someone
It's the best feeling in the world

I start my day with you on my mind
You are there when I open my eyes
You never leave me through the day
You are there still as I close my eyes
At the end of the day
I finish my day with you on my mind
Just like I started it
With you always on my mind

What is love
How do you know what love is
How do you know you love someone
If you are asking these questions
If you are wondering
If you are doubting
You are not in love
For love feels like you
Can conquer the world
Love feels like
Nothing will ever tear you apart
Love feels like
You have wings and can fly
Love feels like
You are invincible
Love feels like nothing else matters
Love feels like you are invincible
That's what love feels like

I am yours
You are mine
There is no one else I want
There is no place I would rather be
But beside you
For a lifetime

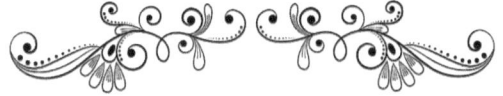

When I see your face
It enlightens mine
When I hear you laugh
It evokes mine
When I hear your voice
It melts my heart
When I feel your touch
It moves my soul

If I give you my heart
What are you going to do with it
Are you going to hold on to it
Are you going to treasure it
Are you going to treat it
Like the most preciouse thing you have
What are you going to do with my heart
If I give it to you

My head is spinning
My mind is racing
With thoughts of you
I can't stop thinking
How fast this is happening
How fast I am falling
Falling for you
Falling deep
Everyday
Deeper
For
You

My heart is searching for you
My soul will find you
For we are meant to be
We are writen in the stars
There is nothing that can keep us apart
For what is meant to be
Will find us
One day my soul will find you
Then we will become
An US

The dapled sun seeps through the canopy
Of the branches intertwined above
Just like your love is seeping into my heart
Through the threads of love
Interlaced over my broken heart
It is seeping in, and my heart
Is begining to break the threads
That once encased my broken heart
For your love is strong and powerful
Entering my heart
Like a strong branch
Begining to grow
Seeping in
Ready to burst through
Into my soul

I look into your eyes
I feel like I'm looking into your soul
For your eyes tell me what you are thinking
Your eyes tell me the story beneath
For your eyes tell me what your heart conseals
Your eyes are the window into your soul
I can't stop looking into your eyes

Even oceans can't keep us apart
For love knows no boundaries
For love knows no distance
For love can swim oceans
Fly through space
Climb mountains
Overcome any obstacle
Placed before it
Love can conquer
More than we imagine

The miles seperate us
But our hearts will always bring us together
For there is no distance
That love can not overcome
Our hearts know no distance
Our love knows no obstacles
For our love knows nothing
But the beat of our two hearts
Beating together as one

Love is an emotion
That has no words
For how can you describe
The most powerful emotion to be felt
It brings the highest of highs
Or bring the lowest of lows
It can feel like Euphoria
Living in Utopia
Or it can bring you down
To the depths of your own hell
Like you are drowning in sorrow
Like there is no tomorrow
There is no one word that can describe
The feelings of love
Love is a feeling only to be described
By the recipient
Of this all encompassing feeling
But when you find it
It's magical

My feet are turning me in the direction of you
My legs keep walking forward
Forward to what my heart desires
Forward to whom my soul knows
Is the only one for me
One step at a time
Each step closer
To you

Love

Where is it

Where do we find it

We are all just vessels looking for love

Looking for that one person to bring comfort

That one person to share our lives with

Share the joys and share the sorrows

That one person to love and be loved

Unconditonally

Love

If only it was easy to be found

Some people have hand held luggage
Some people have a boat load
Just as long as in the end we have matching baggage
Then we can travel this life together

How do you keep someones heart safe
How do you stay friends when they love you
How do you do it without breaking their heart
How do you do it without breaking your own
How do you keep the love of friendship alive
When one wants forever as lovers
When the other wants forever as friends
How do you do it

The sweet rain falls down
Falls like diamonds
Diamonds covering the earth
Drinking in the droplets of love
From above

In a world filled with billons of people
Is it possible to find the one
The one in a billion
The one you were meant for
The one to make your heart beat
The one to make your soul sing
The one to give meaning in your life
The one who makes you smile uncontrollably
That one in a billion
Is it at all possible
To find the one

Dancing with you now
Is like floating in my dreams
Looking from within
A vision that was once a dream
Is now a magical dance of love
Floating across the room
Floating across my heart

A healed heart
Is a strong heart
Full of fresh love
To love like never before
For a healed heart
Knows just what it can endure
Knows how to love
Knows just what true love is
Knows it's worth taking a chance
For a healed heart wants to be loved
And to love again

You fill my days with love
You fill my nights with dreams
You fill my heart with joy
You fill my soul with bliss
You fill my life with serenity
For you are my home
Home for my heart
Home for my soul
Home for love
Home for life

You find that one person
Who completes you
Who makes you feel
Like you are on top of the world
Who makes you feel
Like you can achieve anything
Who makes you feel
Your heart is full
Who makes you forget
Every other relationship you ever had
Who makes you feel
Like your life has just begun
I hope you find that one person

Sometimes I find it hard to breathe
When I think of you
When I think of us together
When I think of a life without you
For the love we share
Is everything I have ever dreamed of
Just thinking of you
My heart skips a beat

With every broken relationship
With every broken heart
A new you is born
The old you is replaced
With a wiser person
A person who knows what they don't want
A person who knows what they do want
Knows their worth
Knows their limits
Knows how to love even deeper
For they know love is beautiful
They know love is worth the chance

I once liked you
You use to be my friend
You used to be the one who made me smile
Now I love you
Now you also make my heart smile
Now you are there for me in every way
Now I can't live without you
I once liked you
Now I love you

Whether you are near me
Or whether you are thousands of miles away
You are never far from me
Near or far
You are never far from my dreams
Near or far
You are never far from my mind
Near or far
You are never far from my heart
Near or far
You are never far from my soul
Near or far
You are never far from me

Looking into your eyes
I see kindness
I see someone wanting to be loved
I see love
Your eyes tell me more
Then your words do
I see the love
I'm just waiting to hear the words
I see
I see this just looking into your eyes
I see the love your eyes want to speak

Unspoken words
Unspoken thoughts
Unspoken love
For your force is constant
For your pull is pulling stong
You are not ready
For my words
For my thoughts
For my love
You may never be ready
So I shall keep my words unspoken
I shall keep my thoughts to myself
I shall keep my love in my heart
Maybe one day
You shall hear my words
Hear my thoughts
Hear my love
Maybe one day you shall feel my love
Maybe one day
You shall be ready
For my love

Do you feel the wind blowing
Do you feel the winds of change
For change is coming
Coming to you
Bringing in a love
Like no other
Blowing out all the old
Blowing out the memories you once had
Blowing in a love you have never felt
Blowing a love directly to your heart
Blowing in a love so pure
A love that will stand
Any winds coming your way

A love like this
Is only seen in print
So how can this love be real
How can we be living this day
And every day
With such joy
With such love
With such happiness
When this type of love
Feels like it's only found
In fairy tales
I look into your eyes
I touch your lips
This is not a fairy tale
You are real
This love is real
We are living this fairy tale
Together
With my prince charming

You were born to shine
Shine bright
You were born to make a change
Change the world
You were born to inspire
Inspire happiness
You were born to show the world
How to love
So shine bright with your love
And show the world why
You were born

I feel like I'm floating
I feel like I'm looking down from above
Looking at a couple whose love
shines for the world to see
A couple that feel so blessed to
have found each other
That they don't mind who sees
their love shinning through
A couple who have been waiting a
life time to find each other
Now we have found each other
I never want to be apart
I never want to let you go
I will be forever grateful that our two worlds
Have collided and allowed us to meet
Allowed us to find love

I've been looking for you
I've been looking for a life time
I will keep looking for you
In this life time and the next
Until I find you
Until my soul has found you
Found the one who makes it complete
For a life without you
Is a life empty
So I shall keep looking
Until I find you

We talk about love
About the love of a life time
About finding that special someone
The one that makes our heart beat
The one who makes life feel better
The one who completes us
Our soul mate
But what about our first love
The one you need to love
Before anyone else
The one you need to look after
The one you need to chersish
The one who needs you the most
YOU
You come first
Don't forget to look after you

Will you catch me
If I fall for you
Or will you let me fall
I want to know you will be there
With open arms
If I fall for you
Maybe I will just take the chance
Maybe I'll grow wings and fly
For the way I feel
I could just spread my wings
And fly
Fly to you

Like, Love, In Love
I like you
I like talking to you
I like going places with you
I like your sense of humour
I love you
I love your eyes
I love your smile
I love your laugh
I'm in love with you
I love your mind
I love your values
I love everything about you
Do you ever stop and think
About the difference
between
LIKE,LOVE,IN LOVE

Love is not about the outside
Love is not about being perfect
No one is perfect
We all have scars
We are all imperfect
Someone who loves you
Will love your scares
For they are what has made you
The amazing person you are
They will love your imperfections
For they too are imperfect
Together you will be imperfectly perfect
Together you will beautiful

I've been travelling this road of hope
Hoping that one day I'd find love
One day I'd find the one who make me feel complete
With all my hopes
With all my dreams
I walked a lonely road
Until I found you along the way
The one who has made my hopes
The one who has made these dreams come true
That road that led me to you
That road that led me home
For you are my home
You complete me
Now when I walk down the road
I walk holding your hand
Leading us home
To where our hearts
Have become one

When love comes along
You are not going to have a choice
It's just going to happen
It's going to find you
Whether you look for it
Or not
Your heart will find love
Before your mind will

I feel your love
It feels like a love sent from the divine
It feels magical
To good to be true
How can someone feel this kind of love
How can this kind of love be real
How can your love for me be everything
I have ever dreamed of
How have you come into my life
And loved me like it's the first time
I have ever felt love
If I am dreaming
Please do not wake me
For I want to feel this love forever

Every tear you have shed
Has been collected
Has been noticed
You have not shed them in vain
For you shall see all your tears
All your heartache
Shall now be returned as love
Returned in a love you have only imagined
A love only you are deserving of
So all those tears
Have not been in vain
For now the tears you shall shed
Shall be in happiness

Your life is a love story
Your love story
For every heartache
Every broken heart
Every pang of love
Everyone who has loved you
Everyone who you have loved
Is the story of your love
Your story is not over
Your story is still been written
Only you have the power to change
The ending
Only you have the power to write
An ending of love
Pick up your pen
And write an ending
No one will ever forget
An ending of true love
Forever love

When I say I love you more
It means
I love you more than yesterday
It means
I'll love you more tomorrow
It means
I love you more than myself
It means
I love you more than you do
It means
I'll love you like there is no tomorrow

Love is worth fighting for
We fight for love every day
If you want it to last
You have to fight for it
Pick up your sword and fight
Fight the good fight
Show them your sword
Show them how hard you are going to fight
Fight for their love
But show them
You are also willing to lay your sword down
If they give up on you
If they are not willing to fight
Just as hard as you

Love is going to come when you least expect it
It is going to tap you on the shoulder
You will be shocked
As you turn around
And realise
Love found you
You can't run from it
You can't ignore it
You have to breathe
Except it is here
And rejoice
That love
Has found you

Our love was fated from the start
Across time
Across the universe
No matter where we have traveled
No matter where we have lived
This love was always destined from above
I feel it in my heart
I feel it in my soul
That you my love
Are the only one for me
The only one ever meant for me
We have been guided to each other
To fulfill a destiny designed to be writen in history
For the love we share
Is unmatched by any other
For it was written in the stars
Fated from the start

I love you more than words can say
How do you tell someone you love them
When the words aren't enough
The words aren't sweet enough
The words only seem to get in the way
When love is soul deep
When the love you feel
Feels like it's going to explode out of your heart
When just the sight of your love
Makes your heart try and beat out of your chest
How can words explain the love
That feels ethereal
How can I tell you I love you
When the words are just not enough